ALASKA'S ARCTIC

TEXT BY JAMES LUKIN AND HILARY HILSCHER
FOREWORD BY EDWARD T. HOPSON, SR.

GRAPHIC ARTS CENTER PUBLISHING COMPANY, PORTLAND, OREGON

International Standard Book Number 1-55868-044-6
Library of Congress Number 91-71080
©MCMXCI by Graphic Arts Center Publishing Company
P.O. Box 10306 • Portland, OR 97210
President • Charles M. Hopkins
Editor-in-Chief • Douglas A. Pfeiffer
Project Manager • Richard L. Owsiany
Managing Editor • Jean Andrews
Designer • Robert Reynolds
Cartographer • Manoa Mapworks, Inc.
Typographer • Harrison Typesetting, Inc.
Color Separations • Wy'East Color, Inc.
Printer • Rono Graphic Communications Co.
Bindery • Lincoln & Allen
Printed in the United States of America

Contents

◄ ◄ ◄ Braided rivers cross the tundra, carrying snowmelt from the great spine of Alaska's Arctic: the Brooks Range. Those who look beyond the frozen winter will find a remarkable landscape, wildlife, and people. ◄ ◄ A winter landscape reveals the outline of a frozen stream. ▲ An Arctic fox. ► The July breakup of sea ice along the Beaufort Sea coast signals the end of winter.

Iḷumutun kaŋiqsiñiaqtuni manna nunakput, Arctic-mik pisuuraŋat apiqsriaqaqtuq kaŋiq-siḷugiḷḷu Iñupiaŋi, pir̄gausiŋat, suli iñuuniaġusiŋat. Pir̄gausiŋisalu iñuuniaġusiŋiḷḷu Iñupiat iḷaupiallaktut mattuma niġrutiŋiññun nunam, nunamullu, taġiumullu, suli tamanna iñuuniaġvigiraqput irrituruaq.

Iñuuniaqapta iñuguġniḷukkama maani nunami siġġaġnapiallaŋaruq. Ataramik aŋuniḷuk-tuaqhutik. Uvva uttaqiyumaŋitkiga taipkua uvlut. Aglaan uvva pir̄gausiŋat Iñupiat suli sivuni-qaŋiñmiuq uvagut iñuuniaġniqput utqutiḷugu pilġusiptiktun nukatpiaġruuŋŋaġma.

Iñupiat pir̄gausiŋat ittuq suli qanukkiataŋ iñuuniaġniŋat qaaŋianiktuami qaitchivḷuni aul-latiksraŋannik iñuuniḷugniġmi pagmapak allaŋŋuqtuami nunaptigni. Uvagut allaŋŋuq-tuksrauvluta aglaan tammautigiŋiḷḷakput akisurualuk pigianiktaqput puqiutiŋanni mattuma nutaaġuqtuam nunam. Uvva allaŋŋuutipta iḷaŋit aŋuniaġniptigni atullasiŋagivut supputit, igni-qutiligaanik umianiŋammiugut, suli sno-go-niŋammiugut. Aglaan taamna sivuniqaŋitchuq, tainnaitkaluaŋŋaġmi, uvagut tammaiñivḷugu pir̄gausiqput. Uvva qutchiksuaġipiallakḷugu quki-givluguunnii manna nuna ittugut. Suli qukigipiallakḷugi iḷisausiavut uvagut kiŋuvaaġiraptigniñ utuqqanaaġiraptigniñ. Tavraasii tainnamik pituksimmatigigivut qaaŋianiktuallu tiki-saaksravullu. Uvva savaktaurugut uumuŋa kamanaqtuamun nunaptignun irrituruamun.

Iñupiat iñuuniŋat tunŋasuuruq uvagut piḷḷaniptigni iñuuvluta nunami suli nunam qaisaksraŋani. Tainnamik qutchiksuaġipiallaguugivut niġrutiŋit, iqaluiḷḷu qaugaiḷḷu qanutchi-payaat katitkaluaġaptigiŋ uvagut iñuggutiksravut niqiksravut. Uvagut taġium siñaaniittuanii Iñupianii, aŋuniaġniŋa aġviġum — uummatiptignun atapiallaktuq pir̄gausiptigni. Tavra itqanaiy-autigivlugu aŋuniaġniksraq, aŋuniaqtuallu, suli autaaġusiaqḷuta aġvallagruaġmata tamarra tamatkua nuimapiallaktut. Iḷuqaiññik isumalaaġutigiruksraurut atautchikun. Aġvallagruaqa-miuna iñuum niġipkaġuugaatigut iluqapta. Aġvallagruaqtuam uuma nalupqinaiġuugai tasama akisuvialukkun aitchuusialgitchugut autaaġusiusiaqaġnialgitchugut suli pir̄gausiqput igliqtil-lugu. Tavraasii tainnamik aġvallagruaqtuam patchisilluataġuugaatigut quvianniqiniaġapta atautchikun iḷitqusiptigni suli Iñupiaguniptigni.

Uvagut Iñupianii suaŋapiallakḷugu inauniptigni taamna suaŋaruaguruq. Una inigikkaqpuut irrituruaq aimaaġvigigikput. Qiñiġaaŋiḷḷu uqaluŋiḷḷu ukua maqpiġaat ikayuġligit iñuich imma allani nunani naakka pir̄gausiñi qiñiqtuaqpata aimaaġviptignik. Tasamma tainnatun kaŋiqsisi-qaġniaqtugut mattuma nunagikkaptaa irrusiŋanik, niġrutiŋiññiglu iñuŋiññiglu. Tainnatun quliagtuaġikaptigiŋ piqatiġiiksiłḷuta gaġġisuurriruq tainnasiq kaŋiqsiñmik maani iñuuruat iḷitqusiŋannik.

Foreword

by Edward T. Hopson, Sr.
Text in Inupiaq and English

A true understanding of the Arctic requires an understanding of my people, their traditions and their culture. The traditions and culture of the Eskimo are a part of the wildlife, the land, the sea, and the Arctic environment. The life that I lived growing up in the Arctic was very harsh. It was a constant struggle to survive. I do not want to go back to those days. Keeping alive the culture of the Inupiat people does not mean we have to live as I did as a boy.

My people's culture has survived because the traditions of the past provide guidance for living in a changing world. We must be adaptable, yet not get lost in the values and technology of the new world. We have adapted our hunting practices to include the use of rifles, motorboats, and snowmobiles. This does not mean, however, that we have lost touch with tradition. We still respect the environment. We respect the lessons of our ancestors and Elders. We are the link between the past and the future. We are the stewards of this great Arctic land.

My people's survival has depended on our ability to live with and from the environment. This brings a deep respect for the mammals, fish, and birds that must be gathered in order for us to survive. For the coastal Inupiat Eskimo, the hunting of the bowhead whale — *aquig* — is the heart of our culture. It is the preparation for the hunt, the hunting, and the sharing of the successful hunt that are important. They must all be considered together. The successful hunt feeds us. The successful hunt affirms our shared values and traditions. The successful hunt gives us reason to celebrate together our spirit and sense of identity.

We Inupiat have a strong sense of place. This place, the Arctic, is home. The pictures and words of this book can help people of other places and cultures share our home. Sharing can help bring understanding of the Arctic's land, wildlife and people. Sharing can bring understanding of the Arctic's spirit.

◄ *The lack of topographic relief on Alaska's Arctic Coastal Plain allows streams to meander, as they do in flat regions everywhere. But "patterned ground" reveals permafrost beneath the surface.*

ARCTIC CIRCLE

ALASKA

CANADA

Fairbanks

Anchorage

Bering Sea

Gulf of Alaska

ARCTIC   OCEAN

Point Barrow

Barrow

PLOVER ISLANDS

Point Franklin

Point Belcher

Cape Simpson

Peard Bay

Dease Inlet

Smith Bay

Cape Halkett

Wainwright

Harrison

Teshekpuk Lake

Bay

Icy Cape

Atqasuk

Nuiqsut

Chukchi

Point Lay

Sea

NATIONAL PETROLEUM RESERVE IN ALASKA

Umiat

Cape Lisburne

Cape Beaufort

LOOKOUT   RIDGE

Meat Mtn x

COLVILLE RIVER

Point Hope

River

NORTH   SLOPE   BOROUGH

ALASKA MARITIME NWR

Black Mtn x

DELONG   MOUNTAINS

B   R   O   O   K   S

Castle Mtn x

Deadlock Mtn

Misheguk Mtn x

NOATAK NATIONAL PRESERVE

Howard Pass

GATES OF THE ARCTIC

MULGRAVE HILLS

Noatak River

NORTHWEST ARCTIC BOROUGH

x Siavlat Mtn

Soakpak Mtn x

x Mt Stuver

Anaktuvuk Pass

CAPE KRUSENSTERN NAT'L MON

Shulakpachak x Pk

ENDICOTT MTS

Mt x Mac Vicar

NATIONAL PARK

Cape Krusenstern

Giav Mtn x

x Mt Doonerak

AND PRESERVE

Diet Ca

Wiseman

▲ *The Trans-Alaska Pipeline disappears over the horizon on its journey from the North Slope south to Valdez. This panoramic image, taken in November along the Dalton Highway, covers about three-quarters of a 360-degree view. To the left the view is east toward the Brooks Range.*

ALASKA'S ARCTIC

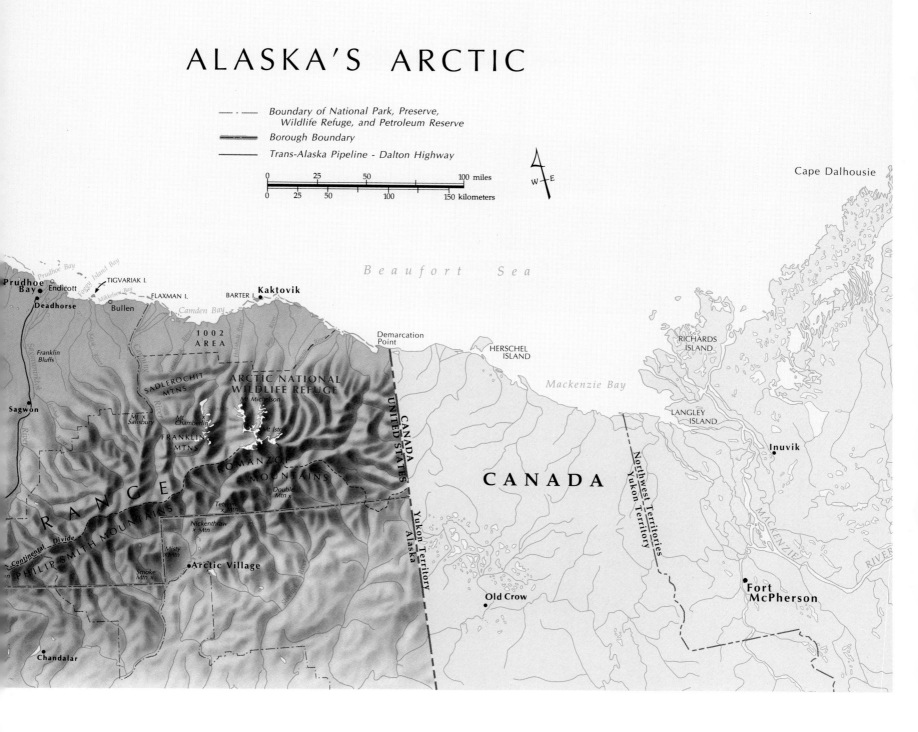

Boundary of National Park, Preserve,
Wildlife Refuge, and Petroleum Reserve

Borough Boundary

Trans-Alaska Pipeline - Dalton Highway

To the right, you can see west along the foothills and the northern edge of the Brooks, while in the middle, the sun sits just above the southern horizon in the upper reaches of the Sagavanirktok River. At this time of year, the sun is barely above the horizon during the brief day.

T he very phrase *Alaska's Arctic* sends a chill of adventure through my spirit. Ever since my introduction to Jack London's tales of the North in my youth, I have been fascinated with cold lands, particularly Alaska. My home state of Connecticut can be cold, but its winters are short-lived. And much to the dismay of a school child, snow does not come often enough to really affect school days. Imagine a place, I thought, where snow is permanent and darkness prevails!

When I first visited the North Slope in June 1974, my vision was quickly changed by the scene that unfolded beneath the plane as we crossed the continental divide, heading north across the Brooks Range. Stretching to the horizon was the great plain of the North Slope, dotted with innumerable lakes and accented by meandering streams and braided rivers. Though some ice remained in lakes and along the rivers, the green-brown landscape contrasted sharply with the ice-locked land of my imaginings. At first glance, this nearly flat landscape could have been mistaken for parts of the Midwest.

In later years, when I visited the region again in my work, I was struck by how much I had missed the first time, when I focused on the breathtaking expanse. Given the chance to see it in all seasons, I began to appreciate its subtleties and the remarkable features clearly distinguishing this region from other parts of the country. I also learned how difficult it is to walk in wet summer tundra. With a close-up view came the realization that you must forget the physical abuse from boggy tundra, hordes of mosquitoes, and bone-chilling cold. You must step back and *experience* the wonder of this mystical place, quite literally at the edge of the world.

Alaska's Arctic is known to most as the North Slope. Even for Alaskans, it is a place few visit; in fact, it is over five hundred miles from where most Alaskans live. While many Americans think of Alaska as a cold and forbidding place meant only for a summer visit, they may be surprised that many Alaskans have a similar view of the North Slope. Nearly half of them live in Anchorage, and to most, the Arctic is as foreign as Anchorage seems to South Carolinians.

Alaska's Arctic is a land of contrasts. It is truly as cold and forbidding a place as most people think: for most of the year, the North Slope is locked in snow and ice. Average temperatures in February are well below 0°F. However, in July, an occasional warm day and the legions of mosquitoes can make one forget all about the extreme cold of the Arctic winter. Summer temperatures have reached the 70s, but normal highs range from the 40s along the coast to the 50s inland. Both Barrow and Barter Island have record-high temperatures of 78°F, with lows approaching minus 60°F.

Stretching north from the crest of the east-west-running Brooks Range to the Arctic Ocean, the North Slope covers roughly eighty-one thousand square miles and derives its name from the fact that it is the "north slope" of the mountains, dropping gradually to the sea. The region stretches over six hundred miles from west to east and is nearly two hundred fifty miles from north to south at its widest point. Remarkably, this vast region holds a mere 14 percent of Alaska's land area but is roughly the size of Kansas. But the North Slope's population is only about six thousand, compared to 2.5 million in Kansas.

America's Arctic mountains, the Brooks Range, form an impressive backdrop to the North Slope. Jutting suddenly from the earth, the essentially treeless mountains reach

Landscape by James Lukin

◄ *Lakes are silhouetted against the tundra, with the Arctic Coast visible beyond. A foot beneath the surface lies a permanently frozen zone as much as two thousand feet deep. Though the region has little precipitation, water cannot penetrate the permafrost, and the flat coastal plain is wet as a result.* ▲ *In a whiteout, the uniform gray-white of sky and snow may cause disorientation.*

heights of over nine thousand feet. With the continental divide running through the range, the streams and rivers on the North Slope flow to the Arctic Ocean.

Unrolling northward like a giant carpet bunched up slightly at the foot of the mountains, the North Slope runs gradually to the sea as a treeless land dominated by permafrost. Permafrost, or permanently frozen ground, is the prime architect of the landscape. The upper foot or so of the ground thaws in summer, and over large areas, this "active layer" is saturated with water. Extending to depths of two thousand feet, permafrost keeps surface water from seeping into the ground, and the annual freeze-thaw cycle in the active layer results in the patterns we see. About half the coastal plain is covered by lakes and ponds—though the region could be considered a desert, with an average annual precipitation of about six or seven inches. The vegetation here is dominated by wet tundra, consisting primarily of sedges, mosses, and grasses. Willows several feet high grow along waterways, but on the tundra, the willows are only inches high.

South toward the mountains, the land's elevation increases almost imperceptibly until drier tundra takes over. In this region, the land is dominated by "moist tundra communities," consisting mainly of cottongrass tussocks with mosses and lichens growing between them. This foothills region has long, low ridges, particularly in the west, and several low mountains, such as Slope Mountain, appear as one approaches the Brooks Range from the north.

While most of the North Slope appears as flat as the Great Plains, in summer one quickly notices that unusual polygonal patterns cover large stretches of terrain, particularly on the coastal plain. Termed "patterned ground," these areas result from "ice wedges" in the soil. Because it gets so cold in the long winter, the ground contracts and cracks, in a process analogous to the cracking of the mud at the bottom of a dried-up pond. These ice wedges grow over many years as meltwater entering the cracks freezes because of the

underlying permafrost, and this growth heaves and reshapes the ground's surface. Patterns of ice wedges create the polygons that proliferate on the coastal plain.

Ice-wedge polygons contribute to the formation of tundra ponds and lakes in a phenomenon unique to permafrost regions. Called the "thaw lake cycle," this process originates as surface water accumulates over ice wedges and in shallow depressions in the polygons, which range from about ten to three hundred feet across. Because of the warming influence of water, the permafrost just under the polygon begins to thaw, increasing the size of the depression. This process continues until the pools in adjacent polygons merge to form a pond, and fairly large lakes may result.

Teshekpuk Lake, southeast of Barrow, is the largest of these thaw lakes at over twenty-five miles long. However, the process does not stop once a lake is formed. As a thaw lake grows, it may encounter a meandering stream, a deeper lake, or even the seashore. The lake will then drain, and a smooth, barren basin remains. It may take several hundred to several thousand years for the cycle to run from formation to draining of a thaw lake. And hundreds to thousands of years more may pass before the basin reverts to tundra as first mosses and then other vegetation appear. With the vegetation again insulating the soil, ice wedges form and polygons reappear.

One interesting feature of thaw lakes on the coastal plain is immediately evident from the air: many are oriented in the same direction. During storms, wind-driven water erodes the shorelines and redeposits sediments, causing the lake to grow in an elongated shape

▲ *The gravel Dalton Highway connecting Prudhoe Bay's oilfields with the continental road system at Livengood, north of Fairbanks, winds out of the Brooks Range onto the North Slope.*

with its long axis perpendicular to the wind. Because the constant winds on the coastal plain prevail from one direction—the northeast—many thaw lakes are oriented along a northwest-southeast line. "Oriented lakes" are so prominent on the coastal plain that early airplane pilots navigated with reference to them.

Other than patterned ground and oriented lakes, what is it that makes this flat landscape so fascinating—besides the fact that it is in the Arctic? It is easy to be moved by scenic wonders such as great mountains and canyons. The Brooks Range, notable for its rugged beauty, does provide such grandeur. But this book concentrates on that part of the North Slope which is not so dramatic: the coastal plain and the gently rolling foothills. A good friend of mine, a biologist who has spent years on the coastal plain, refers to Alaska's Arctic as a place where a person cannot "leave his or her brain on dial tone." He said, "You're not going to be able to go to any particular place and just be struck by the huge awe of it, such as standing at the rim of the Grand Canyon. It's not just one big treasure but lots of little ones. Things aren't going to jump into your eyes; you have to actively seek them out."

These sentiments are echoed by other scientists who have worked on the North Slope. At first, it is hard to understand why they are captivated by their experiences in the Arctic, which is a tough place for the scientist. When you're not freezing in wind-chill factors that seem to approach absolute zero, you're going mad from the mosquitoes swarming around your head or the boggy terrain or tussocks that make every step agony. One scientist, describing his first experience flying over the Arctic National Wildlife Refuge, recounted how he excitedly told his companion how great it would be to spend a month exploring the area. His associate, who had been to the place many times before, thought a minute and responded that it would be interesting, but only for a day or two. But these scientists all smile when they speak of how their experience of the North Slope transcends the tribulations of their field work. I conclude—with great pleasure—that they have a touch of the poet and philosopher in them.

Some spoke of the awe of being totally alone in a landscape so hostile to warm-blooded humans, at being so dependent on one's own resourcefulness for survival.

A field geologist recounted how he was struck by the profusion of summer wildflowers, by the sense of solitude, and by an encounter with a bear that he crossed the tundra to approach because he thought it was the first rock he had seen all day. Some mentioned the fascination with the Arctic that had been engendered in childhood and the excitement of actually visiting those regions. A biologist spoke of the myriad signs in the seemingly featureless winter landscape that reveal the activities of animals or the face of the land and water beneath the white mantle of snow and ice. A Barrow resident spoke of the subtle colors and textures of the Arctic landscape and the feeling of sensory overload experienced upon leaving the nearly overpowering simplicity of the North Slope landscape.

Once we have analyzed this landscape and understood the reasons for its remarkable nature, we must take a step back. The simple beauty and elegance to be discovered in Alaska's Arctic create wonder in those willing to take the time to learn about it. The Inupiat, who have lived in this region for thousands of years, deeply value the rich land which sustains them. As one experiences Alaska's Arctic, appreciation for this unique region can only grow.

▲ *"Patterned ground," the trademark of permafrost etched into the tundra, is created by ice wedges formed in cracks in the ground. These "frost polygons" are prevalent in many areas.*

◄ Cumulus clouds rising over a green sea of vegetation seem more reminiscent of the plains of Kansas than the treeless tundra of Alaska's Arctic, but the solid cement of permafrost is just beneath the surface of the ground. The "pingo" on the horizon has resulted from the natural draining of a lake and the subsequent freezing of the water remaining in the soil under the lake. These circular hills have cores of solid ice and may rise a hundred feet or more above the surrounding terrain. ▲ In the brief Arctic summer, the desolate white of a winter landscape gives way to a sea of plants and innumerable small lakes and ponds that attract breeding birds from the world over.

▲ A winter temperature inversion creates an eerie mirage over an oilfield facility at Prudhoe Bay. This *fata morgana* results from the light passing through layers of warm and cold air. Arctic mirages of this type may enable one to actually see over the horizon. In the summer, the distant ice pack may be reflected in the sky above the horizon—though the ice pack itself cannot be seen directly. ► The sculpted surface of the snow is evidence of the persistent wind, while North Slope oilfield facilities operate in the semi-darkness of a winter day. In December and January when the sun does not rise, an eerie twilight bathes the landscape in pale light for several hours a day.

◄ South from the lake-studded, wet tundra of the coastal plain toward the Brooks Range, the elevation of the land gradually increases and drier tundra appears. The dimpled texture is created by small tussocks formed by sedges such as tufted cottongrass, *Eriophorum vaginatum*.

▲ Production wells on the Slope are drilled from gravel pads, each supporting numerous wells. (Each small building houses a wellhead.) The gravel provides access and a stable surface, as well as insulation to protect the permafrost. Leaving the gravel pad are the flowlines which carry combined oil, water, and gas to processing facilities where the oil is separated for shipment via the Trans-Alaska Pipeline.

▲ Perhaps no Arctic phenomenon is more familiar than the Northern Lights, or *aurora borealis.* Caused by particles from the sun which interact with the earth's magnetic field, these curtains of multi-colored light extend upward from about fifty miles above the earth.
▶ Patterned ground is a distinctive feature of the summer landscape on the North Slope. In the winter, extreme cold causes the soil to contract and fracture. In the spring, cracks fill with water which freezes in the still-cold ground. The resulting ice wedges grow with each year's increment of meltwater, pushing soil upward and toward the center of the polygons. Here, caribou trails skirt the stream bank.

Permafrost, or permanently frozen ground, is the prime architect of the landscape.

◄ Stretching across the tundra like a string of pearls, a "beaded stream" is a series of small ponds connected by flowing water. Again, the architecture of permafrost is at work. As an ice wedge melts from the warmer water flowing over it, slumping and erosion of the soil around the ice wedge creates a depression that fills with water. Such pools, linked by running water, created this beaded stream, located where the wet coastal plain rises to meet the foothills. ▲ The wind and sun create shimmering patterns on coastal plain lakes. ► ► The low winter sun silhouettes buildings outside of Barrow, which at a latitude of over 71 degrees is the northernmost community in Alaska.

▲ Unusually high waves from the Chukchi Sea crash against an ice-encrusted shore after a fall storm. ▶ The character of the Beaufort and Chukchi seas is governed by the nearly year-round presence of ice. Near shore, ice begins to form in September and October and lasts until June or July. In this early November photo, ice has formed along the shore. ▶ ▶ In early exploration on the North Slope, the active layer was sometimes scraped and piled to the side in road construction. The mound in the foreground may have resulted from such activity. The yellow flowers are spotted saxifrage, *Saxifraga hirculis;* the white tufts are cottongrass, *Eriophorum scheuchzeri.*

The simple beauty and elegance to be discovered in Alaska's Arctic create wonder in those willing to take the time to learn about it.

◄ The white tufts of a field of cottongrass grace the tundra. Several species of cottongrass thrive, depending on the moisture content of the tundra; this type, *Eriophorum scheuchzeri,* is common in wet areas. Cottongrass is actually a sedge, not a grass. The two are distinguished by the flowers and the arrangement of leaves on the stem. ▲ An Arctic river follows its braided course to the Beaufort Sea. Even in summer, protected bluffs provide a haven for the remnant snows of winter. Wildlife benefit from the new vegetation which grows after the lingering snow melts. The bluffs are also used by nesting birds and burrowing mammals such as ground squirrels.

▲ Delicate frost crystals several inches high grow from the flat surface of the late March ice in the Beaufort Sea. These crystals owe their shapes to the salt in seawater, which provides the nuclei for the crystals to develop, much like snowflakes. ▶ Breakup on the Beaufort coast is equivalent to spring. As the days of May and June lengthen toward summer solstice, landfast ice along the Beaufort shore begins to decay. Pools of meltwater cover the ice, and the tundra on the adjacent shore wears the drab colors of the Arctic spring in preparation for the burst of green of the brief summer. Driftwood has been carried on the prevailing currents from Canada's Mackenzie River.

◄ A spit of land juts into the Beaufort Sea as the longshore currents arrange the ice in patterns mimicking the spit. The overall circulation of the Beaufort Sea is to the west; however, currents in the shallow nearshore water are often wind-driven in the brief open-water season.
▲ The multi-colored façade of the Franklin Bluffs rises above the Sagavanirktok River's gravel bed about thirty miles south of Prudhoe Bay on the Dalton Highway. According to geologists, the colored sands of the bluffs represent terrain older than the more recent surface of the North Slope. Peregrine falcons, whose numbers have increased dramatically in recent years, find these bluffs suitable for nesting.

▲ Trails worn by thousands of caribou bear witness to migrations to and from wintering areas to the south. Caribou are an essential food source for Inupiat villagers at Anaktuvuk Pass in the Brooks Range.
► A barrier island divides silty water near the coast from clear marine water offshore. Along the Beaufort Sea shore, strings of such islands parallel the coast and create shallow lagoons. During breakup, silty water enters the lagoons from rivers and streams. These gravel and sand islands are only a few feet high, and their shapes are constantly sculpted by wind, waves, ice, and currents. Here, ice is gone from the lagoon in August, while scattered pieces hug the seaward shore.

◄ The annual breakup of ice from the rivers on the North Slope occurs in late May and early June. Even in early July, ice remains as evidence of breakup in the Canning River floodplain. ▲ Arctic pendant grass, *Arctophila fulva*, extends from the margins of a tundra pond and is characterized by its distinctive red leaves. The yellow-green plants here are sedges. Because they provide early feeding habitat, *Arctophila* ponds are important for waterfowl that flock to the region in the spring. ► ► A lead of open water forms in the drifting pack ice. Ice in the Beaufort Sea is found in three zones: landfast ice, drifting pack ice, and the unstable shear zone between them.

You must step back and experience the wonder of this mystical place, quite literally at the edge of the world.

▲ Wind is a constant companion in winter on the North Slope. Here, persistent strong winds carry ribbons of snow from the Franklin Bluffs along the Sagavanirktok River. Frequent winds, along with the extreme cold at Prudhoe Bay, have prompted workers there to refer to 20/20 weather (-20°F with a 20 mph wind, for a wind-chill temperature of -65°F). ▶ A solitary pingo breaks the otherwise-flat landscape. Such ice-cored hills provide the only topographic relief in many parts of the coastal plain. ▶ ▶ Patterned ground is the most prevalent land feature of the coastal plain. At this coastal location, the brownish vegetation could indicate seawater influence.

◄ The eight-hundred-mile-long Trans-Alaska Pipeline reaches across the tundra. Completed in 1977, the pipeline has carried more than eight billion barrels of crude oil from the North Slope oilfields to the ice-free port of Valdez. ▲ The Endicott Development Project, located in the Beaufort Sea east of Prudhoe Bay, is the first offshore oil development in the Arctic. The forty-five-acre Main Production Island shown here supports about fifty wells and the processing facilities needed to produce oil from the sixth-largest oilfield in North America. The gravel causeway connects this island to the ten-acre Satellite Drilling Island, which can support another fifty wells.

▲ A flowering moss campion, *Silene acaulis,* decorates the tundra landscape. A pioneering species on dry sites, moss campion is an example of a cushion plant. During the brief Arctic summer, a virtual symphony of wildflowers plays a remarkable counterpoint to the floral silence of winter. ▶ Small, narrow lakes have been formed in abandoned channels beside this stream, located near the foothills. The tallest woody plants on the Arctic Coastal Plain are the willows that grow along the edge of streams, where they may reach heights of several feet. Elsewhere on the tundra, willows hug the ground and range in height from only a few inches to a foot or so.

Unrolling northward like a giant carpet
bunched up slightly at the foot of the mountains,
the North Slope runs gradually to the sea as a treeless land
dominated by permafrost.

◄ A pingo surrounded by thaw lakes stands sentinel over the lush summer tundra, silent witness to the power of ice to shape the landscape. Lines in the tundra paralleling the lakeshore reveal the movements of caribou. ▲ For a brief time, the tundra vibrates with the colors of fall. Here, the tundra in the foothills of the Brooks Range reaches for the snow-capped summit of one of the highest peaks in the range—Mount Chamberlin at 9,020 feet above sea level. In the twenty-million-acre Arctic National Wildlife Refuge, the Arctic Coastal Plain is at its narrowest, and the high peaks of the Brooks Range dominate the skyline, even from the coast.

▲ A tundra lakeshore is flecked with foam produced by wind and organic matter. The patterned ground of the tundra gives rise to numerous such "thaw lakes." When water collects in a depression, the underlying permafrost thaws more deeply than if water were absent. This creates a small pool which expands as thawing continues around its edges. Eventually, fairly large lakes may develop. All told, thaw lakes cover about half the Arctic Coastal Plain. ▶ Patterns in the foothills result from the work of water and different vegetation. The coarse textures of willow shrubs betray traces of ephemeral streams, while finer textures of the hillsides indicate tussock tundra.

◄ Moving an Arctic drilling rig is no small task, even when roads are available as they are in the Prudhoe Bay oilfield. ▲ An October moon rises over an oil production well pad at the Prudhoe Bay oilfield. "Directional drilling" enables engineers to extract oil from large underground areas using a relatively small surface area. Wells may snake out underground to targets more than two miles laterally and two miles down from the pad. ► ► An unusually calm day quiets the water of two lakes in the moist-tundra foothills of the Brooks Range. Such a tranquil summer scene makes it easy to forget that snowstorms can swirl across the North Slope even in July or August.

◄ While the summer landscape explodes with color, winter presents a far different scene near Prudhoe Bay. A close examination of the winter landscape reveals subtle hues and textures, as well as the myriad shapes of drifted snow with ice. Winter on the Arctic Coast is not all dark. At Barrow, even though the sun sets on November 18 and does not rise for sixty-seven days, twilight brightens the sky at midday for several hours. The length of this sunless period decreases to one day at the Arctic Circle, south of the Brooks Range. ▲ Hoar frost creates intricate, feathery patterns on polargrass, *Arctagrostis latifolia*. Natives used dried grasses as insulation in their fur boots.

▲ Lights from the oil processing facility at the Endicott Development create an other-worldly scene in this remote environment. In the rock formations lying more than ten thousand feet under the surface, the plants and animals from an ancient sea have become the oil of today. ▶ Hoar frost, left by the sometimes persistent fog along the Arctic Coast, encrusts exposed structures such as this pipeline valve. During the depths of a North Slope winter, it can get cold enough to turn metal brittle. To protect production facilities from the ravages of such a hostile environment, buildings enclose many North Slope oilfield operations that would be outdoors elsewhere.

◄ Rising to heights of up to nine thousand feet, the Brooks Range juts abruptly from gently rolling foothills. Here, the plume of snow and clouds over the mountain reveals high winds, while shadows of snow extend on the downwind side of dead vegetation protruding through the November snowpack. ▲ The steeply angled strata of Slope Mountain at the northern fringe of the Brooks Range provide a dramatic backdrop for the Trans-Alaska Pipeline as it heads south for Valdez. An extension of the Rocky Mountain chain, the Brooks offers quite a clear view of the area's geological history. Numerous marine fossils indicate that it was once submerged under an ancient sea.

▲ Built in 1985, the Endicott causeway near Prudhoe Bay extends technology's reach into the Beaufort Sea in the Sagavanirktok River delta. This causeway connects the two Endicott oil production islands with the Prudhoe Bay road system ten miles west and supports the pipeline carrying Endicott oil to the Trans-Alaska Pipeline. Permits for causeways in the Beaufort Sea include provisions for bridges because of concerns for fish. ▶ During July and August, Arctic wildflowers offer a pleasant respite. Arctic poppies, *Papaver* spp., act as solar collection dishes to concentrate the sun's rays, elevating the temperature inside a flower above that of the surrounding air on a sunny day.

◄ Pipelines at Endicott and in other North Slope oilfields are built in zigzag patterns to allow for thermal expansion. ▲ Most of the 415-mile-long Dalton Highway, or "Haul Road," was built in 1974 in only five months to support construction of the Trans-Alaska Pipeline. The road provides the only overland link to the North Slope oilfields. In spite of the advanced technology needed to extract oil from the Arctic, these oilfields could not function without the simplest of mineral resources—gravel—mined from inactive river channels and floodplains. Without gravel, which insulates the permafrost, buildings and vehicles would sink in quagmires of melting, ice-filled soil.

▲ Barrow, with thirty-five hundred residents, perches on the edge of the Arctic Ocean near the northernmost tip of the United States. This primarily Eskimo community is the seat of municipal government for the North Slope Borough. Roughly the size of Oregon, the borough is larger in area than 80 percent of the states in the United States. ▶ An inactive Distant Early Warning (DEW) station sits on the Beaufort Sea coast at Bullen Point. A string of radar installations was built across northern Alaska, Canada, and Greenland in the 1950s during the early days of the Cold War. These DEW stations were designed to warn the United States of a Soviet attack coming over the ice pack.

A biologist spoke of the myriad signs in the seemingly featureless winter landscape that reveal the activities of animals or the face of the land and water beneath the white mantle of snow and ice.

◄ A meandering stream on the coastal plain stands locked in winter ice. Rivers may freeze to the bottom for miles, making the survival of Arctic fishes precarious. Scattered throughout the rivers are deeper spots which do not freeze completely, providing overwintering pools critical to such species as whitefish and char. ▲ In this land of ice and snow buffeted by wind, nature sculpts simple shapes of exquisite beauty, as in snow arranged on blocks of grounded ice near Barter Island. ► ► The braided Canning River forms the western boundary of the Arctic National Wildlife Refuge. The major rivers and streams flow north from the Brooks Range to the Beaufort or Chukchi seas.

▲ Truckers traveling the Dalton Highway between Fairbanks and Prudhoe Bay must brave winter cold and dark. And in summer, the choking dust and roughness of the gravel road make any trip a grueling adventure. ► In summer, the Arctic coastline is the boundary between the warmer land and the very cold water. This proximity results in fog and low clouds. In fact, coastal airports such as Barrow and Deadhorse are frequently closed because fog reduces visibility and ceiling to below the safety point. The Arctic ice pack can be seen in the distance as the July sun warms the air, lifting the fog. ► ► The North Slope tundra often displays strange and interesting patterns.

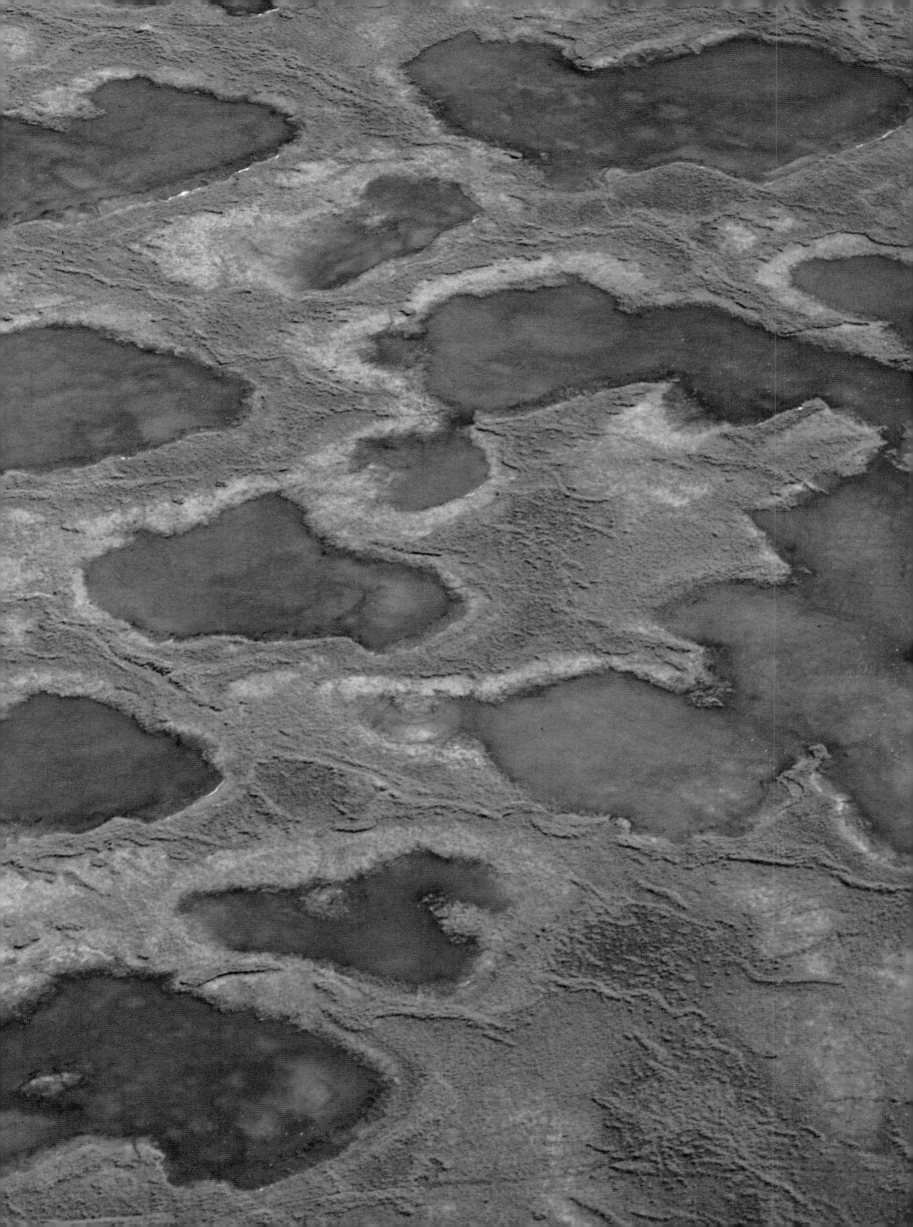

◄ The fiery red Hue Shale is visible in the Ignek Valley between the Sadlerochit and Shublik mountains in the Arctic National Wildlife Refuge (ANWR). The word *Ignek* is derived from the Eskimo word for fire. Some of the rocks exposed in these mountains resemble those yielding oil at Prudhoe Bay, one hundred miles to the northwest. These rocks may extend beneath the coastal plain of ANWR, giving the 1002 Area potential for a major oil find. ▲ Steeply dipping rocks reach from a ridgetop in the mountains in ANWR, south of the coastal plain, indicating that the earth has been deformed. Long ago, the mountains in this region were uplifted above the coastal plain.

▲ At current production levels, North Slope oilfields provide some two million barrels of oil per day, about one-fourth of the United States' domestic oil. These fields include the Kuparuk, Endicott, Lisburne, and Milne Point fields, as well as the giant Prudhoe Bay field, which alone accounts for three-quarters of North Slope oil.
▶ Pan ice in a spring lead in solid ice creates a surreal scene near Peard Bay on the Chukchi Sea coast. Pieces of pan ice are usually not so similar in shape, since wind and currents break them irregularly. So many variables influence ice—its shape, thickness, and stability— that the Inupiaq language has dozens of words for ice and snow.

◄ "Crustose" lichens take hold on rocks in the Kingak Hills in the Sadlerochit Mountains of the Arctic National Wildlife Refuge. Called "crustose" because they form a crust on the rock, these lichens are composed of algae and fungi in a "symbiotic" relationship. ▲ A stream makes its way across the coastal plain near the Prudhoe Bay oilfields. The course of this stream and the small lakes created by abandoned meanders would seem familiar to anyone who has flown over the rivers in the Midwest or on the Great Plains. The green summer tundra with its myriad lakes and streams certainly dispels any belief that the North Slope is a land of perennial ice and snow.

▲ Developed for travel on the tundra where there are no roads to protect the permafrost, Rolligons exert relatively little pressure on the ground. They are able to traverse frozen tundra without damaging the active layer. ► Sparkling diamonds of light burst from windswept snow crystals on lake ice in the weak sunlight of an early winter day near Prudhoe Bay. Unlike the ice-free regions farther south, the coastal areas of the Beaufort and Chukchi seas benefit little in winter from the moderating influence of the ocean. Barrow and Barter Island, on opposite ends of the Beaufort coast, have normal daily highs of about -14°F in February, with extremes ranging to -59°F.

Since moving to Alaska, I have discovered that I truly enjoy winter more than summer, although it seems strange to me that as a member of a warm-blooded species, I would ever find Alaska a hospitable land. After all, human beings are not physically designed for life in the cold. Our pitifully exposed bodies provide essentially no protection, in obvious contrast to the animals adapted to live quite well in the Arctic without the aid of the technology that keeps people alive there. And while the Native people of the Arctic have adapted themselves culturally over the millennia to living in near-perpetual cold and snow, most Americans are ill-prepared for the rigors of such a life.

I've often wondered if it is not because we are so fragile and, underneath it all, so afraid of the cold that we assume that animals living in the Arctic must be struggling to survive. Unfortunately, this anthropomorphic view is a poor basis from which to understand the remarkable adaptations of Arctic wildlife to their environment.

The Arctic surely is not an easy place for wildlife, and far fewer species exist there than in temperate regions. In general terms, the farther one gets from the tropics, the fewer ecological niches, and as a result, the fewer species there are. One reason can be found in the difference in the amount of solar energy available at different latitudes. Moving toward the poles, the length of daylight varies more from day to day, and the solar energy reaching the surface varies greatly from summer to winter. Furthermore, in Arctic regions, the lack of trees creates an essentially two-dimensional world without the many niches of a forest.

As a result, only about one percent of the mammalian species in the world can be found in Alaska's Arctic. And while one hundred or so species of birds come to the North Slope to nest in summer, only about ten actually live there year-round. What most intrigues the biologists who work there is that Arctic conditions tend to simplify biological systems, leaving only the best adapted and most resilient species. And the treeless, nearly flat landscape of the North Slope gives biologists a wide-open view.

The wildlife that use the North Slope either have adapted to year-round life in the Arctic or have adopted migration as a way to take advantage of the brief but highly productive summer. From land mammals such as caribou, muskoxen, moose, wolves, ground squirrels, foxes, and lemmings, to marine mammals such as seals and walruses, the animals of Alaska's Arctic have numerous physiological and behavioral adaptations to the rigors of this extreme environment. And those that migrate to the region in summer to breed or feed have adapted as well. They benefit from the plentiful food and relative lack of predators, and they know when to leave. Birds and whales,  for instance, undertake long-distance migrations to escape the winter while still making the utmost use of the resources of the Arctic during their visits in the summer.

The lemming offers one of the more interesting examples of the fascinating adaptations of resident wildlife on the North Slope. Snow, the ubiquitous substance of the Arctic winter and the symbol of cold to us humans, actually provides a haven for these small mammals, which could not survive exposed to the elements. Capitalizing on the excellent insulating capacity of snow, lemmings burrow under the snow, which also provides them refuge from the Arctic foxes that prey on them. Underneath the snow at the ground surface, the temperature is relatively stable all winter long and can be substantially

Wildlife by James Lukin

◄ *Male polar bears,* Ursus maritimus, *roam the pack ice, hunting for seals. This one, about eight years old, weighs some eight hundred pounds.* ▲ *Snow geese,* Chen caerulescens, *sport neck bands placed by scientists studying the population. Howe Island, near Endicott, hosts the only known snow goose nesting colony in the United States, although many colonies exist in Canada.*

higher than the outside temperature. In fact, snow is a very good insulator, because of air trapped within and between the snow crystals. The so-called "subnivean" temperature keeps lemmings comfortable as they live under the snow, digging nests and tunnels in their subnivean kingdom. At the same time, wind-chill temperatures in the outside air just a foot or two above their heads can drop to -100°F. Thus, in spite of the flat stillness of the winter tundra landscape, remarkable activities are taking place under the snow pack.

The concept that snow is "warm" may seem strange, but mountaineers and back-country skiers who venture out in winter know its value well. Schools on winter survival start out teaching students the rudiments of building a snow shelter, the inside of which can be quite comfortable, even while temperatures outside plunge well below zero.

In addition to the lemming's use of snow for insulation, the animals living in the Arctic have developed insulation of their own. The polar bear is able to stay warm on the Arctic ice pack because of the combination of its insulating fat layer and its air-trapping fur, composed of hollow hairs. The coats of land-dwelling mammals such as Arctic fox and caribou are also extremely effective in warding off even extreme subzero cold. Muskoxen, too, have a remarkably fine insulating hair called "qiviut." Domesticated muskoxen are raised for this underwool, which can be spun into a superior yarn prized for its softness and warmth. And while bird feathers may, at first glance, seem designed only for flight, one of their primary functions is to keep birds warm. Humans have been trying hard with their technology to duplicate the fibers that Arctic-dwelling animals have evolved for defense against the Arctic winter.

When one sees a caribou or a raven, it is easy to understand that their fur and feathers insulate well, but what of their thin legs or the raven's bare feet? Remarkably, the caribou's legs are designed to operate at a temperature as much as 50°F lower than the core body temperature. And the arrangement of blood vessels in the legs allows for heat transfer between the warm arterial blood coming from the heart and the cooler blood returning to the heart in the veins from the feet and lower legs. While existing to some extent in most mammals, this "counter-current" blood circulation is highly developed in the caribou. Birds have similar physiological adaptations to the cold, enabling the raven to

stand motionless for hours on its naked feet.

In summer, the North Slope is quite different. The intensity and persistence of the Arctic summer sun stimulate an explosion of life. Barren tundra turns lush green, and flowering plants, for a brief time, carpet the landscape. Insects flourish. And migrant wildlife from the far reaches of the earth come to give birth, feed, and raise their young. The birds that come to the North in summer provide remarkable stories of migration: an adaptation quite different from the ability to keep warm. Over one hundred species of birds arrive to nest on the Arctic Coastal Plain in spring from wintering ranges as far away as the southern tip of South America. Waterfowl such as snow geese, tundra swans, and brant use the summer tundra for nesting and raising their young. Shorebirds such as plovers, phalaropes, and sand-pipers abound in summer, as do loons and gulls. Predatory jaegers and snowy owls also nest on the coastal plain, their numbers following the cycles of abundance of prey. Arriving in May and June as winter releases its grip, most migrant birds in the Arctic leave again within two or three months, just ahead of the return of the long winter.

Migration is an adaptation also used by some species of fish in North Slope rivers and streams. Take char, for instance. Relatives of the more famous salmon, char have adapted

▲ *The population of muskoxen,* Ovibos moschatus, *on the eastern North Slope now numbers more than five hundred. The Inupiaq word for muskox is* umingmak, *referring to its beard.*

quite well to a fresh-water environment that is locked in ice for as much as nine months of the year. While other fish such as the whitefish have sought winter shelter in deep pools of rivers on the coastal plain, char have migrated all the way up to perennial springs in the foothills of the Brooks Range. Here, the char have established a sort of pecking order to allocate space in the pools, with the younger, smaller fish and the older, larger ones separated. This keeps the younger fish from being eaten by the older ones.

Fish overwintering is a concept that is easily understood, but which nonetheless provides a fascinating story. It illustrates the fact that even adaptation has its risks. As one biologist put it, the habitat of Arctic freshwater fishes can be compared to a large room full of people. With a high ceiling in the summer months, the room provides plenty of space for the occupants. Imagine, however, the ceiling lowering for most of the year and leaving only about five percent of the space, as most rivers and streams freeze completely, except for only deep pools and springs. An exceptionally cold winter can spell trouble for overwintering fish if the ceiling in these pools lowers to the floor.

Of course, land and fresh water are not the only habitats supporting wildlife on the North Slope. Offshore, in the realm of Arctic ice, marine mammals make their living, again providing evidence of the cyclical use of the Arctic by its wildlife. The immense bowhead whale, which is so important to Inupiat culture, is a migrant to the Beaufort Sea. Reaching lengths of sixty-five feet and weighing as much as one ton per foot, these whales spend their winters in the Bering Sea and arrive in the Beaufort in spring, following openings and leads in the ice off the coast at Barrow. They then follow the developing leads east along the coast to the Canadian Beaufort, where they spend the summer feeding. They return to their winter feeding grounds in the fall, migrating back along the Beaufort coast. Their distance offshore depends on ice conditions. The reason for their appearance in the Arctic Ocean is the abundance of small, shrimp-like crustaceans during summer. Bowheads use the great baleen plates that hang from their upper jaws to filter these crustaceans from the water. This baleen provides an additional benefit for the Inupiat whalers, who hunt the bowhead for food and other needs. Natives carve baleen or weave strips into exquisite baskets.

Other whales also frequent the waters of the Beaufort in summer, among them the gray whale and the much smaller beluga, or white whale. Belugas are often found with bowheads on their spring migration into the region from wintering areas to the south. Bearded and ringed seals, as well as walruses, also inhabit the Chukchi and Beaufort seas. These marine mammals provide with their meat and blubber a source of energy for not only the Inupiat, but also for the polar bears of the region.

To truly understand Arctic wildlife, we must first forget the fact that we as humans would quickly die if exposed unprotected to Arctic cold. It is also important to look at wildlife through the eyes of the Inupiat, and not just through the analytical eyes of scientists. Before the arrival of the white man in the Arctic, the Inupiat of Alaska's North Slope depended entirely on hunting for survival. Even now, as the Inupiat live straddling the Western world and their own culture, they continue the subsistence hunting of their ancestors. In such a challenging land, they celebrate the gifts of nature and have developed a unique feeling for the animals that give them sustenance. The Inupiat hunter believes that the animals have given themselves for the Inupiat's survival, and for that the hunter is grateful.

▲ *A cow moose,* Alces alces, *with twin calves crosses the foothills tundra. Moose on the North Slope live primarily along rivers and streams where the willows grow that they favor as food.*

◄ The long hairs on the underside of this muskox hide the "qiviut," a wool which makes an excellent yarn. Uncontrolled hunting once eradicated Alaska's muskoxen, which now number about twenty-five hundred in the state. By the early 1970s, the Alaska Department of Fish and Game had reintroduced the muskox to the North Slope. ▲ A six-hundred-pound bearded seal, *Erignathus barbatus,* plunges into an open lead in the Beaufort Sea. ► ► In a phenomenon known as "predator swamping," female caribou give birth during a brief period, so that more calves are available than predators can take in a short time. This reduces the overall mortality rate of the calves.

◄ A relatively uncommon bird in the Beaufort Sea region, Sabine's gull, *Xema sabini,* migrates from wintering areas off the western coasts of Africa and South America to reach summer breeding areas in Alaska's Arctic. ▲ The breath from a group of Pacific walruses, *Odobenus rosmarus,* creates an eerie fog above their heads along an ice floe in the Chukchi Sea. Most walruses from the Pacific population live in the Bering and Chukchi seas; however, some individuals may range to the east. The Inupiat Eskimos, particularly those on the Chukchi Sea coast, traditionally hunt walrus for meat, blubber, and other needs. The Inupiat carve walrus ivory for sale.

The intensity and persistence of the Arctic summer sun stimulate an explosion of life.

▲ An enthusiastic caribou calf cavorts while its mother seems more concerned with making a living on the tundra. Caribou, *Rangifer tarandus,* which winter in the foothills of the Brooks Range and in the forest to the south, return to the coastal plain to calve in June. Thus, they minimize predation by wolves, which must stay close to their dens in the foothills and mountains to care for their own young. ▶ The predatory gyrfalcon, *Falco rusticolus,* is a relatively common year-round resident of the foothills and mountains in Alaska's Arctic. Many gyrfalcons live along the upper reaches of the Colville River. This young fledgling appears indifferent to summer's abundant insects.

◄ The mountains of the Arctic National Wildlife Refuge provide a spectacular backdrop for this group of caribou. A tight grouping like this indicates that the animals are seeking relief from the legions of insects that harass them in summer. Insect harassment can be a serious problem for caribou, who will even swim out to islands in the nearshore Beaufort Sea to escape the onslaught. ▲ As summer sets in on Alaska's North Slope and the females have given birth, the caribou disperse across the tundra to feed on the spurt of vegetative growth engendered by continuous daylight. Small groups of caribou such as these males can be seen throughout the region.

▲ In summer, a young caribou rests under the pipeline which carries oil from the Endicott Development to the Trans-Alaska Pipeline. Current designs for pipelines such as this one include elevated sections and ramps for caribou passage. The Endicott line was built during winter from a snow and ice pad to protect vegetation and the active layer. ▶ While some birds are abundant on the North Slope in summer, others are less common. The western sandpiper, *Calidris mauri,* here perched on a willow shrub, is sometimes seen on the Beaufort coast during fall migrations from western Alaska across the North Slope and south to southern coastal regions of North America.

◄ The red-necked phalarope, *Phalaropus lobatus,* a shorebird, nests throughout the Arctic, particularly in wet areas of the coastal plain. Unlike most birds, it is the phalarope male, rather than the female, that incubates the eggs on the nest, and the female has brighter plumage than the male. ▲ One of the first shorebirds to arrive in the Arctic in spring, the ruddy turnstone, *Arenaria interpres,* nests on the Beaufort Sea coast, preferring dry locations in areas such as river deltas. In the winter, ruddy turnstones range as far as the southern tip of South America. ► ► After calving, caribou come together in huge "post-calving aggregations," such as here near Prudhoe Bay.

◄ The dark coat of an Arctic fox pup, *Alopex lagopus,* contrasts markedly with its winter white. The ears of the Arctic fox are small, thus minimizing heat loss through its ears. Arctic foxes, which live year-round on the North Slope, benefit from numerous nesting birds in summer, since bird eggs are a favorite meal, as are small mammals. Arctic foxes may be cute, but caution is required: they can carry rabies. ▲ Numerous bird species nest on the North Slope in the brief summer. One attraction is few predators; another is the explosion of insect life when winter finally ends. Migrant birds nest quickly in the Arctic summer, and most leave the region in about two months.

▲ The long-tailed jaeger, *Stercorarius longicaudus,* is an avian predator that visits the North Slope in summer, feeding primarily on lemmings, birds, and voles. These birds winter off the coasts of North and South America and migrate in the spring to the Beaufort Sea region, arriving in May and June. Their preferred breeding habitat appears to be near the northern foothills of the Brooks Range. ▶ The greater white-fronted goose, *Anser albifrons,* is commonly found along the Beaufort Sea coast in summer. After wintering in the valleys and coastal marshes of Texas, Louisiana, California, and Mexico, the white-front migrates north along the Pacific and Central flyways.

The birds that come to the Arctic in summer provide remarkable stories of migration: an adaptation quite different from the ability to keep warm.

◄ A type of sandpiper, the dunlin, *Calidris alpina,* frequents Arctic Alaska in the summer and spends the winter in the South China Sea. After nesting on the tundra, these dunlins move to the coast along the Beaufort Sea, where they gather on mudflats to feed and molt before migrating to their wintering areas. This dunlin is standing on driftwood along the Camden Bay coast. ▲ Perhaps the most spectacularly plumed bird that visits the North Slope, the male king eider, *Somateria spectabilis,* contrasts vividly with the plain brown female. With as many as a million king eiders visiting the region in the summer, they are one of the more abundant bird species found there.

▲ The tundra swan, *Cygnus columbianus,* breeds on Alaska's north coast, where an estimated three to four thousand of these waterfowl nest. Among the first birds to arrive in May, most tundra swans that breed on the Arctic Coast spend the winter along North America's Atlantic Coast. The Mackenzie River valley in Canada's Northwest Territories serves as their migration corridor to Alaska's Arctic. ▶ The preferred nesting habitat of Pacific loons, *Gavia pacifica,* provides an example of adaptation. They nest on islands in large tundra ponds where they are relatively safe from land-based predators. In addition, Pacific loons take flight by running across the surface of the water.

◄ The bowhead whale, *Balaena mysticetus,* fills essential cultural and nutritional needs for the Inupiat. These whales, which can reach sixty-five feet in length, are hunted by the Inupiat as the whales pass near the coast in spring and fall. The International Whaling Commission has established a quota system to control hunting of the endangered bowhead. ▲ Polar bears, *Ursus maritimus,* are feared predators in Alaska's Arctic. They spend most of their time on the pack ice; however, they may range along the coast after landfast ice forms in the fall. The Inupiaq word for polar bear is *nanuk.* ► ► The winter coat of the Arctic fox provides ideal camouflage in the snow.

▲ In a lead in the Arctic ice, a group of bowhead whales, *Balaena mysticetus,* are swimming with a smaller beluga, or white whale, *Delphinapterus leucas.* Bowhead whales migrate into the region in spring, following leads in the ice east from Point Barrow to their summer feeding grounds in the Canadian Beaufort Sea. ► Smaller cousins of the Canada goose, brant, or *Branta bernicla,* feed on aquatic vegetation and prefer to nest on spits, barrier islands, and islands in river deltas, where they are relatively safe from land-based predators such as foxes. ► ► Red-throated loons, *Gavia stellata,* nest on the shores of shallow ponds on the Arctic Coastal Plain.

It is also important to look at wildlife
through the eyes of the Inupiat, and not just
through the . . . eyes of scientists.

◄ Barren ground grizzlies, *Ursus arctos,* live throughout the coastal regions of Alaska's Arctic but are more plentiful in the mountains and foothills. ▲ Common in the region some years, the snowy owl, *Nyctea scandiaca,* usually builds its nest on an elevated patch of tundra so it can watch for prey. Since the snowy owl depends largely on lemmings for food during the summer, the number of owls living on the North Slope varies with the lemming population. Lemmings are noted for explosive population growth followed by a crash, in cycles that range from two to five years. When the lemming numbers are low, the snowy owls range south to the northern tier of states.

▲ Because of the flat, wet nature of the coastal plain and permafrost's proximity to the surface, the Arctic ground squirrel, *Spermophilus undulatus,* digs its burrow in river banks or the sides of small hills or ridges lacking shallow permafrost. For eight months a year, the ground squirrel hibernates to protect itself from the Arctic winter. Unlike the grizzly bear, which is dormant in winter, the ground squirrel is a true hibernator. ▶ The gray wolf, *Canis lupus,* also seeks dry soils for digging its dens, normally in the foothills and mountains. Since wolves prey on caribou, the denning habits of wolves probably help explain why caribou have their young on the coastal plain.

Through history, humans have known Alaska's Arctic as a home, a jobsite, a frontier. In the earliest days, ancient tribes followed the animals of their food supply across the grassland connecting Siberia and Alaska fifty thousand to fifteen thousand years ago. Small groups settled in the Arctic, which nurtured and sustained successive civilizations, culminating in today's indigenous race of Inupiat Eskimo.

The first white men arrived in the late 1830s, exploring and charting the coastline. In the mid- to late 1800s, whalers and traders sought profits—oil and baleen from bowhead whales, and fur from land mammals. Some of these people stayed, becoming the Arctic's first non-Eskimo residents. In 1890, missionary educators moved north to live among the Inupiat; government officials soon followed. Word of the Arctic's great wildlife population spread, and during the 1930s, naturalists and scientists came to study the animals and the land.

The military arrived in 1940, first to explore for oil during World War II, then later to capitalize on the Arctic's important strategic location during the Cold War. In 1968, oil company employees came to develop the resources of North America's largest oilfield. In the 1980s, a new group of adventurers began to visit this extraordinary, vast frontier.

Living there. Foremost among those who live there are the Inupiat, who consider the Arctic their permanent homeland. Most other residents are transient, living in one of the North Slope's eight communities or wilderness for a while—even years—but ultimately moving back south. The contemporary Eskimo lifestyle blends age-old subsistence hunting and fishing with the Western cash economy.

In this still-communal society, sharing is a given. "On the Slope, living is so easy," said a woman from Barrow, now a corporate officer in Anchorage, a city of two hundred fifty thousand. "There, you know everyone; you can borrow anything you need. You'll always have a place to live and food to eat. Up there, you belong."

To understand this closeness among the villagers, it is important to remember that for centuries, Arctic civilizations developed in isolation. People along the coast hunted seals, walruses, and whales; their trading partners in the foothills and mountain passes centered their world around the caribou. When the explorers and whalers arrived,

they found a resourceful culture based on inventive technology and customs.

Kinship formed one of the most important principles of Inupiat society, for those without proper relationships were considered enemies. People believed that human and animal spirit forms reincarnated from one life to the next. Names of recently deceased would be given to newborns, a practice still followed by today's Eskimos and many other cultures as well. The Inupiat developed special rituals around hunting, to ensure that the animal spirits would escape to regenerate and return to once again feed the people.

The first, and perhaps greatest, agents of change for Inupiat culture were the whalers. They brought Western weapons that increased hunting efficiency, and diseases that decimated Eskimo communities. They introduced wage-paying employment and alcohol, new foods, and new family surnames. Their legacy continues today in all facets of Inupiat life. Missionaries and government teachers induced the next changes with programs to improve villagers' health care and to replace their language with English.

People by Hilary Hilscher

◄ *Wearing the traditional* atigi, *or parka, an Inupiat Eskimo woman tracks through wind-sculpted snow along the beach at Barrow. Most of the town's residents enjoy modern amenities such as electricity, water, sewer, and cable TV.* ▲ *Archaeologists have found evidence that Eskimo cultures have lived in the harsh environment of the Arctic Coastal Plain for eleven thousand years.*

Then came the impact of the military: more jobs and wages, and more interaction between Inupiat and Western cultures.

In the past twenty years, two major events occurred which have resulted in greater self-determination by the Inupiat. In 1971, Congress passed the Alaska Native Claims Settlement Act, awarding Alaska's Native peoples land and money through Western-style corporations. More than five thousand northern Inupiat hold shares in the Arctic Slope Regional Corporation. Corporate officers pledge to pursue profitability in a way that "enhances Inupiat culture and economic freedoms."

The North Slope Borough, established in 1972, operates like a county government and is funded primarily by taxes on Arctic oilfield development. A major employer for residents, the borough finances capital projects, operates public services, and supports a locally controlled school district.

Perhaps nowhere in America does "future shock" intrude on daily life as it does for the Arctic Inupiat. Along with the grave social problems confronting all societies today— alcoholism, domestic violence, poverty, disease, and suicide—the Eskimos face an added dilemma of trying to integrate two cultures. They continually seek a balance between Western conveniences and age-old skills, between the English language and Inupiaq, between television programming and traditional values. And the young people especially struggle to merge the teachings of the elders with the demands of the modern world.

While the North Slope's long winter may be "normal" to the Eskimo, it poses a difficult challenge to the psyche and resources of other peoples seeking to live in Alaska's Arctic. The isolation and climate conspire against a positive mental outlook. But Arctic living for the non-Inupiat does offer significant compensation, say those who have moved north. They talk of the restful, pastel hues of sky and snow, and the richness of learning another culture's view of the world. And when summer finally arrives, everyone rallies with boundless energy in the twenty-four-hour sunlight.

"It's hard to remember there's a world outside when you live in Barrow," said a former borough employee. "And when you're away, it's hard to imagine living under Arctic conditions." For some, a rewarding quality of life prevails in these mainly Inupiat com-

munities. The slower pace and a sense of having enough to live well without excess contribute to a stronger sense of self and more genuine interaction among people. "Everyone's presence and participation matters there," mused one former resident. "In the Arctic, human beings still live close to nature's rhythm and order. It's a combination of peacefulness and excitement, and it makes you feel somehow more alive."

Working there. "Commuting" takes on a whole new meaning for one who signs up to work in Arctic oilfields. Most of the Slope's thirty-seven hundred employees commute two hours via jet to the jobsite, then put in "seven twelves" (one week of twelve-hour days) before heading back home. Their days revolve around work schedules and responsibilities. Jobs are absorbing, sometimes demanding, always time consuming. But work is not all there is to life in the "oil patch." There's the adventure of it: experiencing the Arctic firsthand, living an unusual lifestyle, being part of a small group focused on a common purpose. "People on the Slope are really unique individuals," described an oil company biologist. "They wouldn't take a job in the Arctic if they didn't have a bit of pioneer in them." People develop a strong sense of community, making close friendships frequently with people very different from themselves in background and views.

▲ *At Point Hope, traditional grave markers of whale ribs and Christian crosses show the synthesis of old and new beliefs among the Eskimos, who call themselves Inupiat, or "the real people."*

The overall job, of course, is to produce oil. Most workers perform various aspects of this complex task, while others supply support, including vehicle repair, food preparation, office work, and communications. Many workers spend most of their time indoors—working in shirtsleeves despite the frigid air outdoors. Living quarters offer familiar American amenities, from video libraries to exercise facilities.

Many oilfield employees have commuted to the Slope for years. While they may appreciate and enjoy their work, the split lifestyle often takes a toll, particularly on family life. The Slope routine differs from normal life in other ways too, especially when it comes to daily chores. There aren't any. "I rather enjoy being taken care of," quipped one worker. "Here, I don't have to cook, clean up the kitchen, or make my bed."

Along with those who work at the main oilfield developments, others—mainly scientists and researchers—frequently spend time in the field. Geologists, biologists, botanists, and archaeologists seek to discover the Arctic's myriad secrets. They often live close to the land and come away with a taste of how it feels to call the Arctic home.

For all their differences, those who work in the Arctic and those who live there share certain images and knowledge. They are familiar with the region's dancing mirages and haunting Northern Lights. They appreciate the tundra's year-round wildlife; they welcome back its fairweather feathered visitors. And they know, despite all humankind's singular ideas and sophisticated technology, that winter's cold and dark still reign supreme.

Visiting there. Most Arctic visitors want to experience the "Land of the Midnight Sun," so they come during summer. With construction of a hotel in Barrow in 1954, tourism on the North Slope began. More than two hundred visitors came that first season—more than fifty-four hundred came in 1990.

The oilfields, too, draw several thousand visitors each year, who go on oil company VIP trips or organized tours arranged by travel companies. "Three things always wow 'em," related one Prudhoe Bay bus driver, who has been showing folks around for eight years. "They're always amazed at how great the food is, how tidy things look, and how many caribou just hang around everywhere."

With America's growing interest in the environment and wilderness adventure travel, recreational visits to the Arctic have increased dramatically since the mid-1980s. Guides and naturalists lead small groups on backpacking and river rafting expeditions to experience the wildness and the wildlife. One traveler described his experience this way, "At some point you realize how thoroughly miserable you are physically. You're wet and cold and tired and bug-bitten. But then you realize that doesn't matter at all when compared with the tranquility and peace of heart you feel." Another visitor called it "a humbling experience to be human size in such an immeasurable vastness, where nothing familiar exists to help judge scale or distance." Along with those who journey to the Arctic, many "armchair travelers" also value the region deeply. Though some may never see it in person, they, too, thrill to the idea of this last grand frontier—that speaks to the explorer in all of us.

Humans continue to tell the Arctic's story. From our perspectives as resident, worker, and visitor, we describe its dynamic land and wildlife. Yes, it's cold. But it's also beautiful. The Arctic is filled with contrasts, abundance, and opportunities—examining these carefully can help us better understand the choices facing us in this valuable region. Issues of land use, subsistence, development, and protection deserve our best attention and collective wisdom. For these will help determine the next chapter for Alaska's Arctic.

▲ *Eskimo dancing, initially banned by the churches in the late 1800s, has made a resurgence as village elders teach children the rhythmic, symbolic movements of ancient legends and lessons.*

▲ Twenty-four hours a day, highly trained technicians at the Endicott Oil Development monitor and control production via state-of-the-art computers. Most "oil patch" employees work week on/week off, spending seven days living in company housing on the North Slope, then flying to other locations in Alaska for their week off. ▶ Eskimo youngsters learn early to help harvest bowhead whales. This little fellow grips a *tuggaun*, the tool for slicing the whales' two-inch-thick *maktak* (skin) and the twelve inches of blubber underneath. He wears the traditional white parka of the hunters and has store-bought boots—a common blend of both traditional and modern clothing.

◄ The Arctic Slope Regional Corporation's Barrow headquarters won first place in a national architectural-design competition. In 1971, the Alaska Native Claims Settlement Act awarded Alaska's Eskimos, Indians, and Aleuts nearly one billion dollars and forty-four million acres of land. The settlement was distributed through Western-style corporations in which Natives are shareholders. ▲ A Wainwright home sports caribou hides, Halloween decorations, and a campaign poster for mayor of the North Slope Borough, the local government that covers ninety thousand square miles. It provides public services, finances capital projects, and employs eleven hundred residents.

The contemporary Eskimo lifestyle blends age-old subsistence hunting and fishing with the Western cash economy.

▲ An Eskimo woman drags home a spotted seal, which will provide meat, oil, and materials for clothing and household implements. About 80 percent of North Slope families obtain some of their food from subsistence hunting and fishing—a practice which not only puts protein on the table, but fulfills cultural and spiritual purposes as well. Sharing food is especially important in this traditionally communal society. ▶ An *umiaq*—large, open boat made of skins of bearded seal or *ugruk*—waits by an open lead, a water highway created by retreating and shifting pack ice. The *umiaq* can be maneuvered silently and easily through frigid Arctic currents in pursuit of marine mammals.

◄ Point Hope residents begin to cut up a spring-caught bowhead whale, with portions distributed according to custom among whaling crew, elders, and other villagers. Some meat is put away for holiday festivals; some is consumed—raw or cooked—by everyone at water's edge. Whaling captains hold an honored rank in Inupiat society, for tradition says that the whale gives itself only to a worthy hunter.
▲ A fisheries biologist analyzes young whitefish as part of an annual fish-monitoring program along the Beaufort Sea coast. Scientists are attempting to determine if the gravel causeway that leads to the Endicott oilfield has any effect on migratory fish populations.

▲ Multiple layers of clothing and face masks help protect against the North Slope's bone-gripping wind-chill factor, which can reach as low as -100°F. While some oilfield employees do experience the extremes of the Arctic environment, most work indoors in climate-controlled buildings, complete with gourmet cafeterias, exercise facilities, libraries, auditoriums, and satellite television. "Slope life" carries an air of unreality about it: no children, no senior citizens, no pets, few women. Home, even for Natives who work in the oilfields, is always somewhere else. ▶ Dwarfed by drill rig machinery, workers on the rig floor change pipe and drill bits during the drilling process.

◄ A swimming pool at Wainwright's Alak School provides recreation for children and a reservoir for fire fighters. In 1894, the federal government took over from missionaries the education of North Slope Natives for grades 1-8. After eighth grade, children either left school or went to boarding schools elsewhere. In 1975, the North Slope Borough established its own school district and constructed local schools through high school. ▲ Arctic Slope Regional Corporation board members operate in two worlds: they dress in Western suits and speak Inupiaq, participate in subsistence activities and close million-dollar deals, and manage corporations and keep cultural traditions.

▲ The Commission on Inupiat History, Language, and Culture of the North Slope Borough works to preserve traditional music, once forbidden by church and school officials. Eskimo drums, constructed of seal skin stretched tightly over circular wooden frames, are played by striking the frame with a wooden stick. ▶ Crafts from natural materials have provided an important source of cash to North Slope Eskimos since the 1870s. For example, the coastal people created these boats using *baleen*, a hard, black, fibrous substance found inside the mouths of bowhead whales. The inland Inupiat, however, utilize the caribou's fur, skin, bones, and antlers for their artwork.

◄ Satellite communications connect the industry and villages of Alaska's North Slope with the outside world. Modern communications technology carries information ranging from oilfield data and weather forecasts to college extension courses and medical consultation. Many Inupiat consider TV entertainment a mixed blessing, however, as they strive to perpetuate their traditional language and values in the face of Western-culture programming. ▲ On the snow-packed runway at Barrow, an Eskimo bush pilot prepares to hook up a heater to warm her Cessna 207's engine. Small planes are the taxicabs of Alaska's Arctic, where communities are not connected by road.

▲ In 1973, twenty-seven Barrow families established the permanent village of Nuiqsut on an old fishing site along the Colville River. Now home to 320 residents, mainly Inupiat, the village has wood-frame houses typical of other Arctic communities. The popular conception of an "igloo" comes from the style of snow huts hunters built for temporary use away from the village. ▶ The quick-flowing Hulahula River, frothy gray with glacial silt, offers kayakers and rafters a spectacular ride through the Arctic National Wildlife Refuge. Guides and naturalists lead summer backpacking and float trips throughout the twenty-million-acre refuge of mountains and coastal tundra plains.

In the Arctic, human beings still live close to nature's rhythm and order. It's a combination of peacefulness and excitement, and it makes you feel somehow more alive.

◄ Caught through winter ice, Colville River cisco, oil-rich whitefish, freeze immediately on the snow. The Inupiat consider it a delicacy to eat thin slices of the raw, frozen fish dipped in seal oil. Fish caught during the summer are hung out to dry in the constant Arctic breeze.
▲ After chopping small holes in the Colville River ice, this fisherman will stretch a gill net in the water below, anchoring the net on the surface of the ice. Behind him stands an "iron dog" of the north, the snowmobile, which replaced dog teams in the 1960s. Prior to that, Eskimos used sled dogs for transporting people and goods in winter. Today, snowmobiles rival cars and trucks for in-town winter travel.

▲ Fresh fruit attracts Barrow residents celebrating June's *Nalukataq,*
the whale-catch festival, which draws everyone to the beach for
feasting, playing games, dancing, and visiting. ▶ A *Nalukataq* reveler
is tossed high in the air from a sealskin blanket. Eskimo gatherings
often feature traditional competitions, like the knuckle hop, seal walk,
finger pull, and one- and two-foot high kick—sports now popularized
by international Arctic Winter Games. ▶ ▶ An Inupiat hunter picks
his way through pressure ridges of ice along the Chukchi coast. Most
hunters still wear the white parka to camouflage themselves, and
fasten their mittens with a yarn shoulder yoke to insure against loss.

◄ Workers practice the deployment of oil-containment booms near Endicott, the first offshore development in the Beaufort Sea. The oil industry is continually upgrading its spill response capability with new technology, increased planning, and frequent spill response exercises. This addresses, in part, concerns of North Slope Natives about the possible effects of offshore exploration and development on the subsistence hunting so important in their culture. ▲ During the summer, many villagers move to temporary fish camps along the rivers and coast. Whole families work together harvesting fish according to Nature's clock—sleeping when tired, eating when hungry.

Foremost among those who live there are the Inupiat, who consider the Arctic their permanent homeland. Most other residents are transient . . . ultimately moving back south.

▲ Many an Eskimo baby is still carried in age-old "piggy-backed" fashion inside its mother's parka, with small face peering out from the soft fur ruff of the hood. ▶ Like children everywhere, Inupiat children are outdoors to play at the first hint of warm weather. They grow up in one giant, extended family, for all North Slope Inupiat are related to each other in one way or another through kinship or quasi-family relationships. Peoples of other cultures now also live in Arctic communities: the borough's resident population is 72 percent Inupiat, 19 percent white, 3 percent Filipino, 2 percent other Alaska Native or American Indian, and 1 percent each Black and Hispanic.

Graphic Arts Center Publishing Company would like to thank BP Exploration (Alaska) Inc. for its generous support in making possible this book by providing the necessary access to the remote Alaska's Arctic for the following photographers: Bill Hess, Fred Hirschmann, Danny Lehman, David Predeger, Patrick Prosser, John W. Warden, and Myron Wright. We also appreciate the numerous other photographers who supplied countless contributing photography for this book.

Following is a list of the photographers and the page numbers where their images may be found: • Steven C. Amstrup, pages 11, 32, 40-41, 71, 81, 86, 91, 103, 115; • Walt Anderson, page 79; • Chris Arend, pages 129, 132, 141, 142; • Randy Brandon/ Third Eye Photography, page 42; • Danny Daniels, page 138; • David Eves, pages 128, 131, 134, 135, 136, Back Cover D; • Albert A. Dekin, Jr., page 127; • Mark Fraker, pages 17, 107, 152-153; • Robert Hartzler, page 90; • Bill Hess, pages 150, 151, 156; • Fred Hirschmann, pages 24-25, 26, 27, 126, 133, 140, 143, 145, 148, 149, 157, 158, 159; • Yogi Kaufman, pages 101, 110, 119, 123, 125; • Charles Krebs/ Allstock, page 106; • Danny Lehman, Cover, pages 2, 6, 14, 15, 18, 19, 28-29, 30, 35, 38, 43, 44-45, 48, 50, 54, 56-57, 58, 67, 70, 72-73, 74, 75, 76-77, 78, 80, 83, 84, 85, 88, 98, 99, 102, 124, 146; • National Marine Mammal Laboratory/David Withrow, page 118; • David Predeger, pages 31, 33, 96, 109, 111, 112; • Patrick Prosser, pages 4, 13, 39, 46, 47, 55, 59, 60, 61, 64, 66, 92-93, 100, 130, 137, 154, Back Cover A; • David R. Schmidt, pages 89, 95, 122; • Jeff Schultz, page 68; • Tim Thompson, page 139; • John N. Trent, page 114; • John N. Trent/Alaska Department of Fish and Game, Back Cover C; • Declan Troy, page 94; • Tom Walker, pages 108, 120-121, 147; • Ned E. Walsh, Sr., page 20, Back Cover E; • John W. Warden, pages 1, 5, 10, 21, 22, 23, 34, 36, 37, 49, 52, 53, 65, 69, 104-105, 113, 144, 155, 160, Back Cover B; • Art Wolfe, page 87; • Myron Wright, pages 8-9, 12, 16, 51, 62, 63, 82, 97, 116-117.

For cooperation and assistance in checking facts to maintain the accuracy of the text and captions, special thanks go to the following organizations and individuals: Alaska Department of Fish and Game, Fairbanks office; Alaska Flyers; Steven C. Amstrup of the U.S. Fish and Wildlife Service; Christine Boyd of Visible Ink, Inc. (Inupiaq typeset-ting); BP Exploration (Alaska) Inc.: Cindy Bailey, Debra Beaubien, Anne Brown, Christopher Herlugson, Roger Herrera, and Steven Taylor; Flossie Crestman of the Arctic Slope Regional Corporation; Jana Harcharek of the North Slope Borough; David Harding; Miriam Hilscher; Gary Hufford of the National Weather Service; Neil Johannsen; Stephen Johnson of LGL Limited; LGL Alaska Research Associates, Inc.: Mark Miller, Robert Pollard, and Shannon Shamburger; Jay D. McKendrick of the University of Alaska, Fairbanks, Agriculture and Forestry Experiment Station, Palmer Research Center; Roger Post of the Alaska Department of Fish and Game; Susan Ruddy; David R. Schmidt of Dames and Moore, Inc.; Robert Senner of Robert Senner & Company; and Declan Troy of Troy Environmental Research Associates.

To the North Slope's vast landscape and abundant wildlife, its resourceful Natives and fascinated visitors, the analytical scientists and undaunted explorers, we say thank you. Each has contributed to our knowledge and understanding of this unique, little-traveled part of the world called Alaska's Arctic.

Thanks *from the Editors*

◄ *The North Slope Borough's eighteen hundred students, like these Wainwright girls, learn Arctic survival skills and academic subjects in the classroom. The Inupiaq language has been part of the curriculum since 1971.* ▲ *A bush plane seems lost above an endless sea of clouds over the coastal plain.* ► ► *Water—frozen or liquid—is an important landscape architect of the Arctic.*